I Drink Beauty From Any Cup

poems by
Linda Zralek

I Drink Beauty from Any Cup
poems by Linda Zralek
Copyright © 2015 Jim Zralek

distributed by Ingram Books and published by idjc press
www.idjc.org

also available as an e-book

ISBN 978-1-937081-38-6

Publisher's Notes:

The poems of *I Drink From Any Cup* are presented in the order chosen by Linda's beloved, Jim Zralek. His arrangement is an impressive work of understanding, and I think the reader will agree that it brings to the collection a truly invitational flow which a chronological rendering may not have offered. Where Linda noted dates of composition these are given discreetly.

The poems are also given here in differing fonts in an effort to be faithful to how Linda recorded them over the years, settling on **Tahoma**, *Lucida Calligraphy*, Papyrus, Bradley Hand, Ariel Narrow, *Informal Roman*, Andy, Franklin Gothic Book, and Georgia.

Feast well at this table of the poetry of Linda Zralek. It is an honor to help make her poems available.

Rev. Steve Wolf, idjc press, steve@idjc.info

I Drink Beauty From Any Cup

INTRODUCTION

During the 2013 Christmas season our son Stephen asked us to share our reflections on what makes a meaningful life. Linda offered several ideas, one of which was this paragraph:

I Drink Beauty From Any Cup That's Offered *is a poem I wrote many years ago. To notice and to appreciate beauty is as important as breathing to me. Simple beauty, everyday beauty. The beauty of nature, of poetry, music, art, the beauty of Marlowe and Owen and all children, the beauty in the goodness of those I love and in others I barely know. I drink it all up and I am always grateful.*

This book of poems, *I Drink Beauty From Any Cup,* is the revelation of Linda's most private deep thoughts, emotions, and inspirations. In her humility she would hesitate to let others read her poems. She showed me only one of them. Whether it was spring's first jonquils, giggling grandchildren, a breeze on the screened-in porch, or the smell of coffee, they all primed the pump within her and began the flow of poetry. After living with her for forty-four years I suspect the pump produces water from heaven.

May you treasure these brief revelations of the soul of someone precious to me, my sons and their families, dear friends, and many others as you also drink from the cup.

Jim Zralek

Nashville, Tennessee

Leaving Saint Thomas

The great, wide circles
      of one small life

The pebble tossed into
      the still pond

Thrown, sewn, pitched,
      spent, given ---- yes,
         given

From the shore out
      to unknown depths
         circles return ---
            abundant gifts and loves
             received

A multiplying
      wildly beyond the
         small stone
            tossed

September 1998

5

Morning Gifts

waking up when my rested body is ready
lying next to the one who shares
   my heart and my life
cool breezes flowing throughout our room
lovely patterns of sunlight and shadow on the blinds
bird songs
warm water on my face
pulling on shorts and a light shirt
walking out onto the porch
   stretching my arms wide
      inhaling and embracing a new day
my sacred morning walk
   feeling the strength and agility of my body
all the holy sights along the way
   sunlight, sparkling dew, freshly woven spider webs,
   rippling creek, shafts of light streaming through tall
   trees, magnolia blossoms that intoxicate me, hills
   and trees and trees and more trees, frisky dogs,
   blue birds and chipmunks, a red-tail hawk and
   HOME
the smell of coffee brewing
the delight of that first cup
hot oatmeal with plump blueberries
sharing the porch, the paper, the pleasures with Jim
always, the awareness of my loving family
   and the communities that give me life and hope

HOW DOES THE CREATURE GIVE THANKS ...

LAST LAP
FLOATING ON MY BACK

Is it anything like this
O Great Hawk ----
To be held carefully
By wind waves
To float with the currents
Where there is no gravity, no fear
Only the open meadows of blue sky
And puffy white clouds

I am a small canoe
On the Ontanaugan near Watersmeat
It's late afternoon on a hot, clear day
I've been on this river since morning
Singing and laughing, sharing jokes and food
Now I'm lazy --- just a soft sweep
On the right, then on the left
Coming near the end
And stretching out the pleasures
As I float by

I wonder
Could this be Paradise

Down to the River

I know this trail
I know where I'm going

Down to the river
for another christening

Maybe the others didn't take

I've heard that practice
makes perfect

True perhaps
with much of life

But not with good-byes

A Morning in February

It is deadly still
And deadly gray
Nothing is swaying
Nothing is trembling

Steel limbs, spread against
A steely sky,
Suggest a mourning
That is private and deep

Across the yard
Near the creek's edge
I spot three jonquils
Small, foolish sparks of light

I wonder
If I could build
A fire
Would I?

I love the March sky
when it can't decide what it wants to do

One minute it's playful
like a child discovering new toys
then it's fierce and angry
like a jilted lover

Now, as blue
as a Jamaican bay
moments ago
it was a steely gray blanket

It's March ---we're in for
a wild ride

Oh God

You take my breath away
Your beauty is everywhere
The soft, subtle explosion of
dogwood and redbud
the shimmering, shy
newness of green leaves

If I were a prisoner of war
locked in a dark room
for seven years
Would I be able to
remember today

The harsh, hard winter is
passed and I can
hardly recall it

Don't ever let me forget April

Spring broke out in Nashville
this week
war broke out in Baghdad

HOW, how can this be ---
everything in me asks this stupid question

It gets harder and harder
to live the questions ---

Everything means more

On our jumbo TV screens
in our sports bars and comfy dens
we watch our smart bombs do dumb things---
horrible things

"Shock and awe" our political leaders call it
and in the bars, folks order another beer
and say they're relieved the basketball tournament
wasn't canceled --- they need some break from
this war --- it's too much for them

What kind of people are we
I don't think we're bad people
but God, surely we're better than this

March 21, 2003

May Day

I drink beauty
  From any cup that's offered

Sometimes I sip slowly
  Sometimes I gulp it down

I find the cup
  Is usually overflowing

And always I am
  Wonder-filled

No Regrets

I made the "mistake"

early on

of adoring my children

Without fanfare,

in deepest   silence

without ceremony

or priest

the vows were made---

to love, to cherish

to adore

oh yes, and to enjoy

Regrets?

Not a single one.

Portland

I'm pretending Summer

hasn't even begun.

You'll be leaving in July –

maybe my heart won't

hurt so much

if I think it's still Spring.

June 2002

It Could Happen

I bury my face
In a cluster of lilacs
Inhaling deeply
And wondering
About all the beauty
Swimming into my nose

I could die of an overdose
I could go crazy
I could have a head full
Of pollen and perfume

I could waste all my days
Like the flowers

April 2007

Lilacs

She was ahead of me -
Didn't even see me,
But I saw her

She wandered off the street
And moved toward the yard
Where the lilacs bloomed

Tenderly she held the clusters
of blossoms - -cupped them
in her hands and drank in
their fragrance – with delight
and pleasure

Later, as we walked and talked
I heard of a long-ago romance
when a young lover
had wooed her with lilacs.

Ah such delight and pleasure-
that quick flight from scent
to memory
that tender embrace of lilac
blossoms
and the undying joy of
young love

INTERPLAY

A patch of blue sky
swims below me

Looking down, I see
the tops of trees

Stately, steady creatures
flow and ripple with delight

Today, Monet paints
in our backyard creek

TEARS

The rocks must
have cried all
through the night

Their tears, still
fresh, glisten
without shame
in this morning's
sunlight

GRACE

The tall trees
who've danced with
the wind
since they were
young
now sway with
grace
as God sighs

AFTER RAIN

You are the deep spring
The constant, the ever-flowing
Keeping us alive
Filling us with music
Carving into our rocky crusts
Quenching our deepest thirsts
Bathing us clean
That we might someday
Sparkle

My Sons

Clay, soft and wet
set here before me
no form I see
only possibility

My hands, new
to this experience, touch
and hold this piece
of earth
this piece of mystery

How will we be
together--- my touch
my shaping and molding
and this gift before me

The wheel will spin
the fire will burn

To Parents

Let them melt your heart

They will, for certain, break your heart

But a heart that has been melted

Won't be shattered or destroyed

However, it will bleed

BIRTHDAY

It was a fine spring day
sunny, as I recall,
and on that sun-filled day
we, who thought we knew
the meanings of
joy, of goodness, of love,
we were given a precious gift
a child, a boy, a son

Now, that boy is a man
and for thirty-five years
he has filled our lives with
joy, and goodness and love

A sunny day, Stephen,
the day you were born !
A brighter world ever since

June 13, 2007

BRIAN

He was born December 3rd
Feast of Francis Xavier
A fiery Jesuit saint

We nearly named him
Daniel
After Berrigan and Ellsberg
Two of today's brave men

But he was BRIAN
Brown-eyed and beautiful
Named for no one
His own person then and
Now

BRIAN
Loved, enjoyed
Cherished, respected and admired
Beyond all words
Then and
Now

December 2005

I strongly suspected
I pretty much knew
That I would love you.
But what I could not
Foresee
Was how much --

I never envisioned
The countless ways
You would bring me joy and
Delight into my life.

Marlowe

Where have you come from,

Little One?

Streams from the Czech Republic, Russia and Ireland,

form the deep river sparkling in your dark eyes.

Branches from England, Lithuania and Scotland

shape the tree that flowers into your sweet smile.

Sunlight and moonbeams from Chicago and Hardinsburg,

Jacksonville and Whidbey Island are the jewels in your tiny hands.

Twinkling stars and rainbows, dewdrops and birdsongs from

Nashville make the music that now beats in your precious heart.

From the four corners of the world

From heaven's dizzying heights and the oceans' blue depths

From the honorable lives of everyday people

From the dreams of lovers and the hopes of dreamers

From two loving hearts whose love conceived you

From the Great Spirit who breathes life into you

You, Little One,

You come from LOVE.

Owen's Ode

O, Owen

O, what a gift you are
O, what joy you bring
O, how we love you

O, yes, you are a Child of the Universe
O, yes, you are part of the Great Circle of Life

> An O has no beginning
> no top, no bottom
> no right or left
> only the   widest   embrace
> that welcomes all

All the sweat and dreams from generations past
Every star and dewdrop, every earthworm and child
> of the here and now
> each vision and invention
> of all that one day will be
You, Owen, Precious Boy,
> hold our past, our present, our future

May goodness inspire you
May beauty stir your soul
May wisdom and gladness guide your steps
May you abide in the LOVE
> that has no beginning or ending
And, always, may you live with that Great Circle
> that embraces you and embraces all

An Autumn Walk

I almost always know
    God's closeness—hardly
        ever know God's distance

Oh, I often know my own
    hard heart, my deaf ear
        my stubborn, proud ways

But, God --- God never budges

October 2002

An Autumn Scene

Who undressed you
      my friend?
Last week you stood tall
      adorned in a shimmering golden gown
Now a ring of crumpled leaves
      encircles you
Naked and exposed
      you simply stand there

Ah, the seasons ---
      will they always
           have their way
               with us?

September Hawk

What is it
up there
that keeps you
up there

A force invisible
to us
upholds
and propels you

With no movement
on your part
you are indeed
unflappable

And I quietly
ponder the power
of such utter
trust

September 2009

December Deer

They prance across
the road and into
the meadow

Their white flags
flying high
don't signal surrender
only playfulness
and delight

I stop to watch
and maybe stay
too long

I want them to
feel safe
and to know my joy

But they are wild things
and for so long
I've been tame

December 2008

DAYS OF CHRISTMAS

we knew we had a week's worth
seven beautifully wrapped gifts
some plans were made
some of the hours were spoken for
much of the time was liquid
and flowed slowly into surprising pools

oh, we worked and cleaned and shopped
we did, we gave all we could
but the graces of sweet love and deep peace
were gifts, pure gifts
and so were the two deer
who wandered into our yard
with eyes full of wonder and blessing

I've been down
Some awful roads

I let my heart
Draw the map

And ended up nowhere

I've been down
Some awesome roads

I let my heart
Draw the map

And I'm still traveling

Summer 2002

Know ? NO ! she says ---
I can't know God
we can't--- really
fully know God

But, I ask,
don't we catch glimpses,
hear rumors,
see signs and wonders

Don't we, now and then,
touch the hem
of her garment

October 2002

PROMISED LAND

Several days ago
I stood in awe
Watching a spider
Weave her web

With courage and intensity
She defied the laws of gravity
To create her masterpiece

On sunlit mornings
I took delight in
That delicate, shimmering tapestry
Amazed at the magic and the majesty

But, today, a moth
Caught in that web
Caught my eye

And for a few moments
We were both trapped ----
His fragile wings
Held by silken threads
Beat frantically to be free
He struggled, then seemed to surrender

Respectful of Nature's ways
I cringed with helpless indecision
Then, in a moment's flash
I saw the moth had not yielded
And the web was badly worn

I reached to free my weakened friend
Unlocking his chains and letting him rest on my arm
Briefly, I connected with his frailty
        and felt his strength
My flesh became a safe place for him to be
And to be set free

Then, life took flight
Here in this plot of the Promised Land
Where everything is held together
Within a wondrous web

Little Hummer

O little hummer
I saw you zooming in
Hungry and eager to nurse

Sadness filled me
When I saw what you saw
Our garden gone to seed
With only withered tits
On limp reeds

No milk here
Sweet bird
But I know
Yes, I know
You will find
Other mothers

Bonnie

I guess you could
call her a visitor
she comes three or four
times a year
stays a few days or
a few weeks
then returns to her
home

Precious beyond words
trusting and loving
To my heart
she's not a visitor
there, she's an abider

Wild Child

I cannot imagine your
   earliest days
Where were you born
   Who was your mother
   Did she care for you
   Did she try
Did you run away
   Were you afraid
   Did you cry

We met so soon after
   your rescue
I remember your eyes
   longing to trust and
   aching to belong

Now we walk together
   a loose leash connecting us
And on some sunlight mornings
   dew drops sparkle like
   diamonds on the tip of
   your sweet snout

Finding a Piece of Driftwood in Oregon

Of course, you began in the sea
The womb of all life
But, you are tree, hardened wood
Once a part of this solid rock
With roots and branches

I hold you now, recently found and still damp
Smooth and worn, peaceful in my hand
I wonder how you returned to the sea, and
How many times you drowned, and
How you found your way to this beach

You have weathered it all
Sun, wind, waves and sleet
Did you enjoy standing upright
How long were you at sea
Did you ever dream of finding me

high tide

the sea
the sky
the night
the sand
all become one

only a few rocks
that jut high
some sea otters
still frolicking
and a beach fire
that's smoldering
remain distinct

beginnings and endings
start to blur
it's easy
to lose oneself
here

July 2010

Even Then

I don't always see
The great hawk
flying above me

Can't be spending
all my time looking
at the sky

Yet, when I'm busy
or preoccupied,
Even when I've been
gazing   downward
I've caught sight of
those broad wings-
shadows floating
across the field

And even then
I know
I'm not alone.

MORNING

In total silence
They appeared
Prancing across the morning dew

They stopped so suddenly
As if a signal had been given –
And looked my way

Frozen in stillness and awe
Motionless except for my throbbing heart
I greeted each one

Enough, someone must have said
And in a wink, the trio
Dashed toward the creek
Then on into the dark woods

My thanks for your visit
May all your travels be
So safe and lovely

July 2003

Sunday Morning

With the first crack
Of light
The first hint
Of a new day
I heard a small voice
Outside my window
Chirp
With great excitement
And gratitude

"For me, for me, for me"

How could I stay in bed

Just a sip
Just to dip
The tip of my tongue
Into something wet.

Some nights
I wake with
The whole Mojave desert
In my mouth.

And I wonder
Where is the water-
the living water
That was promised

I haven't written a poem
in years
And there were these words about a drought

I guess any trickle can quench

After attending part of a poetry Retreat at Pennuel Ridge
– Nevin Trammel
November 2010

Watering Plants

I watered my plants this morning.
    It seems they've been abandoned by their mother.

And if it weren't for the garden hose
    and a small amount of my time and attention,

they would all be dead. It feels good to be
    part of something that keeps something alive

that in turn helps keep something else alive.

Just moments ago, I experienced this satisfaction
    as I watched a delicate butterfly

dance around my plants, as I saw her
    flit in and out of the blossoms, and as I sensed

her drunken delight. A little time, attention and water,
    some blossoms and

butterfies, LIFE and a joyful heart!

July 18, 2007

The Trees, the Dog, and Me

The Maple Tree stood there
Her golden leaves
Enjoying the morning's
Golden rays.

She's like my old dog
Who knows beyond knowing
That I can't resist-
The look, the rolling over
And the turning rub.

I wonder about the
One we call Love
And how much beauty
And joy
Love lavishes upon us

Perhaps
We're hard
To resist too.

For My Friend
Mary Oliver

This great ocean
It's called loss
And grief and death

And, yes, it's called
Life

It is our common christening
Where tears are shed
Or not shed
Where we drown
A million times

Only to find
We've been invited
To float

November 13, 2006

PRAYER

Hopkins writes
The heart rears wings

I know this to be true

This I also know
The heart rears arms

And we
Through our helpless
Prayerful love
For those who are hurting
We wrap our heart's arms
Around them
And we hold them close

Sometimes
This is all we can do

Brenda's Mother

look at the skin
of that old man
brittle and dark

he stands not so
straight any more

but always and always
his arms reach out
and up
he knows life's seasons

the great hawk
circles above him
and he says
yes, oh yes

January 14, 2003

Evening Prayer

More resounding
than the words
I mumbled
were my desperate
fears and longings

O Heart of my own heart
what big ears you have

September 2009

We talk about
God
As though we know
What we're talking about

I do... perhaps
You do, too

In truth,
All I can do
Is use words to
Describe the LOVE
My heart has
Come to know

CPSIA information can be obtained at www.ICGtesting.com
Printed in the USA
LVOW08s0354010616

490729LV00001B/3/P